Gently

Stasia Hudak

BookLeaf Publishing

India | USA | UK

Presentation by *BookLeaf Publishing*

Web: www.bookleafpub.com

E-mail: info@bookleafpub.com

ISBN: 9789357215671

First edition 2022

*For the best sister in the world, Daria, who
is my everything.*

ACKNOWLEDGEMENT

To my parents, who have listened to far too many ramblings. To Katie Lade, who pulls me out of my head and makes adult life bearable. To my grandparents, who have always supported me. To my sisters, who had the (dis)pleasure of growing up with me. To my professors at Grace College, who encouraged me to continue writing. To myself, for believing in me.

PREFACE

I started writing poetry when I was 13. We'd just moved to the middle of nowhere, and I had no friends and no way to process everything that happened to me. 9 years later, I'm still writing poetry to cope. It's messy and imperfect, but I hope that when people read my poems, they'll know it's okay to be messy and imperfect too. Growth isn't linear, and it's better to do something badly than not to do it at all. And above all? Be gentle with yourself. You deserve that much.

Float

Water fills my ears slowly
Then sloshes away
I drift up and down
Buoyed by a lazy wave

Arms spread out
Eyes trained on a cloud
I wish I could stay here
Where every sound

Is a muffled rushing
Joining the blanket of gray
Washing over me
Freeing me from space

It's peaceful here
I don't even exist
Moving without effort
Time is irrelevant

Waves carry me
From life's endless worries
I can rest here
There is no need to hurry

The tug of time normally
Pulls me from place to place
I'm released when I'm here
Able to breathe in its wake

Exhausted, I float
Void of any sensation
Pain has no meaning
I give in to temptation

No vision, no tension
No heaviness or burden
I weigh nothing here
I revel in the curtain

Drawn over my eyes
And muffling my ears
The gentle tug of water
Soothes aching fears

I could stay here forever
Completely free
But there's a splash
To my left, suddenly

I am jerked away
By a sharp, urgent voice
Vision rushes back
I have no choice

Time snaps its leash
Weight settles like a cloak
The mist recedes
And I wish I could float

Box Of Dreams

"It's not safe," they say
Their hands over mine
"It's not safe," they repeat
And they guide my

Small hands towards a lock
Cold metal was forced
Between fingers gripped tight
"Don't fight it, it will be alright."

Tears roll slowly down
My rosy pink face
One step backward
But the result was the same

Touch that burned
Touch that bruised
Nails carving crescents
As they force me to

Lock with my own hands
The box with my heart
"It's okay," they soothe
"It'll tear you apart."

Sobbing, I pull away
They grab my chin
They make me watch
Smiling, as they begin

To suffocate the oxygen
Straight from the chest
Everything slows down
My heart begins to rest

"Isn't this better?"
They ask as I gasp
"Isn't this better?"
As they pull out an axe

They remind me it's logical
To have a quick and easy death
I stare at the lump of matter
There is now nothing left

Tears dry my cheeks
Blood splatters white lace
I wield the ax impassively
They applaud my strength

"So rational," "So wise,"
I am a member at long last
A child genius who saw reason
And put her youth to death

And it was by my own hand
So I can have no other to blame
That would be childish
And my maturity is famed

I am wise beyond my years
Quiet, well-spoken, and brave
A paragon of virtue
And so mature for my age

But sometimes I return
To the room of my first test
I stare at the chambers where
They drained the life from my chest

I can almost envision it
It almost shone with passion
I can feel the phantom fingers
Dragging me toward ashes

They called the fire logic
They called the axe reason
My box was a prison
And they were giving me freedom

There is nothing left now
Of my box of dreams
I would attempt to mourn it

But I no longer feel anything

Health Advisory

It can't be health that matters
When you encourage me to starve
Objectively, that's detrimental
But for me, it's not self-harm

Because pain comes second
Since I'm fat and ugly
It's better to be sick
Than to have no one want me

I know I'm solely perceived
As being far too much
I am not the object of anything
Aside from disgust

I cut calorie after calorie
Find the strength to starve
"I'm disgusting by existing,
Self-control isn't that hard."

I lose weight to gain it
I start over again and again
I ignore the warning signs
I only matter if I'm thin

"You can't really be trying,
Or otherwise, you'd succeed."
"You're just being lazy.
Fat girls can't have an ED."

I despair of ever reaching
The limit where I can consider
Myself as someone beautiful
I just need to be thinner

I rest my forehead against glass
And stare into soulless eyes
I've lost the girl beyond the clothes
As I sought to shrink my size

I want to rediscover she
Who spun silver threads into stars
I spend less time hating
And more time finding my heart

I discover why I struggle
To regulate my feeling
Why I gained weight to start with
Why I self-soothe with eating

And I become aware
As I learn to love myself
That society is not concerned
With fixing my poor health

It isn't about longevity
Or the effects of my BMI
If that were the case,
People would encourage me to thrive

But my lack of well-being
Is not the reason why
Society only shows fat people
As those to change or hide

My existence challenges
The lens we all must accept
I in myself am audacity
If I see myself as more than fat

Because if I did find beauty
In the journey of my health
I could be free of other's approval
To finally love myself

And freedom from constraint
To grow apart from prescription
Is something very dangerous
Because others might just listen

We might pursue happiness
Whatever form that might take
But that doesn't make money

And that's really what's at stake

Our bodies are just pawn
In some corporation's game
They market it as health
But they're the ones who gain

I love seeing people happy
When they work out at the gym
I love seeing people happy
When they love their soul within

But finding inner peace
Isn't something you can sell
So they'll keep pushing tangible
Ways to improve ourselves

So, yes, I want to lose weight
But not at the expense of my mind
I'm healing from inside
It's okay to take your time

Legacy

What once was burning anger
Now is just the ashes of numb
I pass through empty houses
From which no soul may come
A gray coverlet of fog
Has muffled the world outside
Fingers grasp for purchase
To wrench teardrops from my eyes

But there is nothing left to give
I am a limp and broken thing
Dust gathers on the throne
Where I was once queen
Idle fingers trace patterns
Over diamonds and gems
Disturbing desolation
From claiming its own end

The suffocating musk of grief
Forces in with every labored breath
Lungs clench and gasp in effort
To filter oxygen from death
Each inhale is a prayer
That this will be the last
Each exhale is a promise

This spectre has not passed

Sparks had assaulted tapestries
Flames licked up stone walls
In rage had brewed clarity
Scorching meaning from it all
Tales of grandeur, tolls of ruin
Indifferent fire consumed with greed
When all had been devoured
Left in the ashes was just me

I sit beside the ghost of embers
Now crumbled into char and coal
Spring has faded fast away
In autumn's rule, I will grow
A fixture of this castle now
Are the tangles of my grief
Stretched into ivy, hungry
That it may find relief

And I am nothing but shadow
Haunting the halls of my reign
Where spring had danced now
Grief chokes out a narrative of pain
Now only these bones remain
Rejected and brittle and lost
Emotion has come in with the tide
And it ebbs with heavy cost

One day, I may seek to leave
And crunch through morning's frost
Find the beauty in the numbness
Dance with the coverlet of loss
But the day has not come
Where I can abandon this throne
If I were to leave it forever
I would be the only one to know

I was once a queen

The Girl With The Stars In Her Eyes

Constellations span her eyes
As vast as a galaxy
Starlight shimmers in her gaze
Enchants me into fantasy

Born of streams of moonlight
Birthed of sparkling stardust
A swirl of enchanted midnights,
Morning red and golden dusk

The depth of the sky
Is reflected in her eyes
She breathes out sunsets
She exhales the sunrise

Worlds burst into motion
From the words she speaks
Swirling into timeless being
Each one is perfectly unique

Girl of constellations
If only I could stay
And watch your fingers weave
Tapestries from space

I wish I could exist here
And escape this torment
Of knowing I must give up
Dancing in your orbit

Let me be a planet twirling
Forever in outer space
Even make me into dust
Just please, let me stay

This is all that matters
Swirl of colors, sparkling light
She is beauty, she is all
She is morning, she is night

Let me stay

Imposter Syndrome

Doubt creeps into my mind
Looking over the top of his glasses
He opens up my laptop
And sitting down, he begins to access
Every instance of failure
From the hard drive of my brain
He chuckles as he reads reports
And redownloads all my pain
He taps his fingers on my desk
And launches a presentation
He clicks on "Start the show"
And lectures on my degradation
"Silly girl, you're not so smart
These reviews were just mere luck
Oh my, please, did you really think
Those files weren't corrupt?"
Success has fallen in your lap
You really don't deserve it
You have no talents or real skills
You're a failure of a person
So please, honey, take a seat
Don't try, it's quite embarrassing
Don't make me laugh, it's by mere chance
You've not made a mess of things
I close my eyes, block my ears

Close the laptop, leave the room
But nothing can stop the voice I hear
His condescending tone of doom
He takes over what was my office
Props his feet up on my desk
He scrutinizes my every movement
Giving me no time to rest
"Triple-check this, you silly girl,"
He says with a wave of his hand
"This is nowhere near enough,"
He says, issuing another demand
I take the files, finish the job
I wish so sincerely I could leave
But where on earth could I even go
When the voice inside is me?

I Wish You Knew

Dearest soul, maybe soon you'll see
You don't have to keep on pretending
That you're fine, that you don't need help
It's okay to just be yourself

Dearest soul, don't fight back tears
It's okay to sob, to show your fear
I'll never judge you for red eyes
If it's what you need, then please just cry

Dearest soul, I hope you know
There are those who love you so
They want to know who you are
I know being open is so very hard

Dearest soul, no one can be perfect
But friend please know, you are so worth it
We want you here, flaws and all
I want to catch you when you fall

Dearest soul, you've put on a mask
But I see you shining through the cracks
If you need it, you can hide your face
I'll wait over here if you need some space

Dearest soul, when you break down
I'm not afraid; I'm still around
And if you lash out at me in fear
I won't run away; I'll still be here

Dearest soul, you are worth the fight
Call me when you can't sleep at night
You make my world so much better
I can't even express it in this letter

Dearest soul, I just wish you knew
You're so beautiful when you're you
But I know it takes more than friends
To put to rest the voices in your head

Sleeping On Gravestones

Autumn leaves cascade to the ground
Skittering, scraping across concrete
Knees shift slightly on damp dirt
Head bowed to seasons drifting past me

Forehead resting against cool marble
I marvel at its stability and strength
Fingers trace over carved-out lines
I pretend enough pressure can erase

Greyness blankets the world
A colorless coverlet blanketing change
When bleak is finally pulled back
My eyes will burn from the color of pain

Numbness creeps over my skin
Fettering me to my desolate home
Bony fingers grapple for my heart
Night claims sky and with it, my bones

Hands pry my body from chilled stone
Shaking, slapping stiff frozen skin
It's spring out there, don't you know
It's time for you to begin again

Nothing even remains here, you say
He abandoned this place long before you
Time may have frozen you to this place
But it's time to thaw, to start anew

You haul me up, lead me away
Leaves crunch under sleeping feet
Unrelentingly towed towards iron gates
Moving so I don't have a chance to think

Sticks snap under sneakers worn through
Jean brushes against slabs of stone
Ears sting against the biting of the wind
You drag me away from my home

Worn jacket snagging on cold metal
I force open red, swollen eyes
But though I am blinded, I accept
That I must leave before I die

Thank you.

Cautionary Tale

There once did live a young queen
Feet dancing through grass
And stone and over riverbanks
No hardship could long last
Smiles swooped the path
That hummingbirds might take
Blossoms burst from fingertips
Spring sprouted in her wake

Fervently I wish I might
Be permitted to reach and weave
Intermingle caution with blissfulness
Cast even a thread of forewarning
But spring heeds no remembrance
Of that from which it comes
She slipped from summer's inferno
Into autumn's deadened dusk

Mamaw

You think you're unimportant
And that nobody knows your pain
That what you've done is not enough
All you can see are the mistakes

But I see something different
When you come into my mind
I think of the grandma who loves me
And who's supportive and kind

I think of all of the past
And everything you've done
Those memories are so sweet
Like candy or a cinnamon bun

I see you watching me play
With toys that you gave
I see a beautiful counselor
Reminding me to behave

I remember a playmate at the park
Who spent time coloring with me
Or when we prayed before bed
After watching TV

And all of the times you've said
"I love you", because I know its true
All of those little things you've bought me
But don't you know that I love you for you?

I hope you always know I love you
Because you've always been there
Not just because of what you've done for me
My faithful prayer warrior, my fearsome mama
bear

Whether it's quizzing, school, or life
No matter what I'm going through
You're always there for me
And I'll always be there for you

So whenever you feel sad, or old, or unimportant
Because you're not as young as you used to be,
Remember you have a little princess
And she thinks that you're her queen

I love you, Mamaw

Falling

Falling through my fingertips
I watch my energy slip
I sit down

Vaporizing into wind
I lose sight of me again
I don't care

Swirling through what we call life
Catching and reflecting light
I just float

Sliding pieces into place
I feel like I just might faint
I pass out

Summoning a bit of strength
Just to feel it ebb away
I am numb

Wishing I was like the breeze
Mother Nature, carry me
I am done

The Cold Is Home

Thank God, she's gone
They whisper as I turn my back
I slip out the door into the frigid night
I pretend their voices were too quiet
Or that I am oblivious to whom they refer to
I am not oblivious. I know.
I know they mean me as I retreat
My feet weaving paths in freshly fallen snow
Branches creak from the weight
Of unexpected burden piled high on slight
branches
The bustle of the night fades from earshot
And the cold air stings my already reddened
cheeks
The trees block some of winter's blessing
but nothing can keep my legs from going numb
As I scrabble across the log spanning a crystal
creek
Shelter appears through the trees, my colorless
home
Waving welcome with shutters clapping against
its windows
It's cold inside, not much warmer than the
sparkling snow

But as I lay curled in bed and feel teardrops
freeze
I don't mind it because this cold belongs to me

Best Friends

Straw blonde hair and a watery gaze
Playing tag and watching Cyberchase
So many years and outdoor playdates
Now your tired face is just a haze

Long black hair and light brown eyes
A tender heart that never died
I was yours and you were mine
Until we drifted apart with time

Chocolate curls and tan brown skin
One day out and the next day in
Dance and clubs and camp and quiz
Your voice is always in my head

Hair that flowed out like the sea
I never could really let you see
We're so different in what we believe
Maybe someday, we'll agree

You wanted a life on center stage
I know we both made mistakes
We both had a part to play
In why the curtain closed that day

You all made me who I am today
Through all the joy and all the pain
We may now be in a different place
But there was a time when I did say,

You are my best friend

Trigger Warning

Fingers tap with bruising force
Rubbing skin raw with friction
Crescent moons carved in skin
Scratching scars of repetition

Humming under the surface
Buzzing faintly in numb ears
A single claw dragging away
Leaving rivulets of fear

Drops of blood well up slowly
Steadily spilling their way down
Glassy eyes stare into space
Ears filled with a rushing sound

Tension slowly ebbs away
Relief laps at a body spent
Stinging blossoms into clarity
As mania at last relents

More Magical Than Me

I hope you're happy
Arms wrapped around her
Like you never held me
I hope you're happy
Staring into crystal eyes
Endless like the sea

I hope you're happy
Going on adventures
When I had no energy
I hope you're happy
Being with someone
More magical than me

Because the stars shine
In her eyes
Because the trees wave
Branches in time
To the way she moves
With endless grace
A thousand tales to be told
Through her warm embrace

And I know she's a wonderful soul
And I know she's helping you grow

Into a maker of maps
Charting the expanse of the sea
She is the epitome
Of everything you need
And I know that together
You will map the mountains
And dance with trees
You'll soar with eagles
And float on the breeze

I know she is the person for you
And I know you'll be dancing through
Stories you could have never foretold
Sunsets you could have never been shown

And I'm happy, that you're not alone
But it's also hard sometimes to know
That we were made so very differently
And she is far more magical than I will ever be

Your Theatricality

You took my youth
And made it your own
Shredding it to pieces
To fit a body wholly grown
You denied me my birthright
To make mistakes, to cry
You battered my heart
And soothed bruises with lies

Masks of logic
Masks of ice
To hide your possession
A smoke screen
For a magician
Hiding his transgressions
When I came to
The show was over
I was no longer me
Iron heart bound inside
A soft smile hiding
Your theatricality

I never got to express
To cry and laugh and rage

You were the director
The producer managing onstage
You denied me my humanity
My youth, my growth, my depth
You ordered me back to my mark
So I could run it all over again

Masks so stoic
Of self-control
So you never really see
A washed-up actor on the stage
Hiding right behind me
When I saw the strings
The years I lost
I was no longer me
Tangled and numb
In the control of
Your theatricality

Something Else Entirely

I feel nothing
The world passes by
A barely discernable buzz
Of words and sounds
And lights and blurs
I idly wonder
What I would need
To do in order to join it
Fingers outstretched
Riding atop of waves
Invisible to the human eye
I see life between blinks
Snapshots catalogued
Into an analysis
That never has any
Practical application
And I wish I could
Put down my clipboard
And step inside
Mouth numbed by cotton
I tiredly wonder what
Makes everyone so alive?
What am I missing
As I exist in this world
And yet, not of?

Was it something I did?
Or was I born this way?
Is this something
I could ever change?
Could I step inside
Feel the bass thrumming
And feel the beat
Of a thousand clapping hands?
Could I taste colors
So vivid and bright
I could never discern them all?
Could I smell cinnamon
And cloves and vanilla
And feel instantly at home?
Are these sensations --
Are they life?
Would these feelings
Be enough to make me
Feel whole?
Is it something else entirely?
Motivation, passion,
An underlying sense of purpose?
Is it the grand total
Of a lifetime of decisions
Weighed on a scale
Against you in your coffin?
Is it something else entirely?
How can I know?
How can I know what life

Really, truly is?
I'm here, but I don't feel it
I don't feel alive
Is there something I'm missing?
Something that will make the silence
Feel less oppressive against
Ears long-filled with nothing?
Something that will change
The direction of static
Thrumming restlessly against
Bare skin, past the point
Of eternal numbing?
Is there something that will make
Blackness stop oozing
Into every available pore?
Is there something that will
Make these feelings come readily
To the forefront of my chest?
Something that will make
This tension finally release?
Would that be what we call peace?
Or is it something else entirely?
Could I know what it's like
To be open and to communicate
Freely and without reservation?
To hope and dream like I did
When I was a girl, without hesitation?
Is that what life really is?
Are these questions just futile wonderings?

What if we'd never been created?
What if the world had never been formed?
This existence we so easily call life
Could just as easily have never been, right?
So, what is the purpose of it all?
Is there meaning here, to find?
Is there something I was born to do?
Or am I just here, passing time
Endlessly until I finally get to die?
I wish I could float along the river of time
Effortlessly supported by the buoyancy
Of a force moving toward a destination
I wish I could find the ocean holding
All the knowledge of the world
And I could drown in it, becoming one
With questions and theories and ideas
Indistinguishable from total understanding
I wish I could know everything
I wish my mind was a sponge and time
Was irrelevant to my insatiable need
To devour ideas and thoughts
And connections and wanderings
But it is not irrelevant
It ticks by, forever and ever
Until it doesn't someday
When will that day come?
Is that day what life is about?
Or is it about something else entirely?
I'll never have the answer

And that's something that depresses me
I just wish someone could let me know
If it's about watching through shuttered eyes
If it's about pursuing some far-off prize
If I'm just wasting my entire life
Or if it's about something else entirely.

Gentle And Passionate

These are what I wish I knew
Before the age of 22
These are what I wish I learned
I know them now that I've been burned

Don't be afraid to take up space
Don't be afraid to leave with grace
Don't be afraid to be yourself
Don't be afraid to ask for help

Don't stay for those who think you're less
Or for those you feel you must impress
Don't give the precious gift of stress
To those who spurn your gentleness

Ask to be seen for what you do
It's not too much to just be you
Think your life decisions through
And trust what you decide to do

You are amazing, you are kind
It's not prideful to recognize
That your hopefulness is a gift
For those who choose to accept it

You'll gain scars from your life
From every battle, every fight
They're not something you deserve
You should never have been hurt

You are strong, little Stasia
But it's okay to be weak
You are gentle and passionate
And you are a beautiful thing

Stand By You

When the sky comes falling down
I'll come for you, my friend
Please don't take my silence
As a lack of care, instead

Understand I'm doing my best
To make sure you're safe
I made it on my own but
I want to know that you're okay

Words aren't always my friend
I struggle to know what to say
But even though I feel lost
For you, I will always stay

You may never know this poem
Is actually about you
You'll probably never read it
But knowledge doesn't change the truth

I'll sit with you through heaviness
Even if I can't take your pain
You don't have to say anything
My presence will stay the same

And you don't have to heal
Any faster than you feel able
Growth isn't a straight line
It's okay to be unstable

I can't give much myself
As I'm trying to heal too
But I can give you my support
I'll always stand by you

Recede

He feels unheard
So he talks even louder
Hiding insecurities
By joking around and
Who sees his soul?
Who hears his cry for help?
Do they know who he is?
Does he even know himself?

Sometimes we hide so well
We end up hiding from ourselves
We don't know what we need
So we let ourselves recede
We fall farther and farther back
Behind an ever-consuming mask

She's the good child
And she's always around
Never disagrees
Never stands her ground
She's afraid to fight
Afraid to disappoint
So she slips away
She forgets her own voice

One thing we forget
And it's so very sad
We're all painfully human
Underneath our masks
They may be embedded
Habits run deep
We've been trained to display
What other people want to see

And yet our mask doesn't
Have to last forever
Sometimes it just takes
A kind word to let it be severed

To pull off the mask
And let us see
Your beautiful self
Finally set free

Be Gentle

You don't have to be perfect
It's okay to make mistakes
You don't have to life in guilt
You don't have to be afraid

I'll be here when you lose control
When you say things you'll regret
My love for you is not fragile
You can get out of your head

I'm not going to leave you
When you let yourself feel
Your emotions aren't a burden
Your feelings are real

So please, dear friend, be gentle
You deserve to feel love
You are perfect as you are
You are more than enough